I Can Add

Press out stickers, moisten, and place them on the pages where they belong.

page 4

page 12

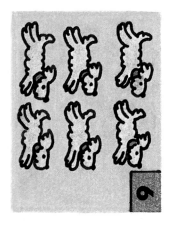

page 5

page 17

Count the objects in each row. Write the number on the line.

How many?

1 2 3 4 5 6 7 8 9 10

Read the words. Look at the pictures. Write the number in each box.

How many 🦁 ?

2

How many more come?

1

How many in all?

3

How many?

How many more come?

How many in all?

Skill: understanding the addition process

Read the words. Look at the pictures. Write the number in each box.

How many 🐢 ?

How many more come?

How many in all?

How many 🦉 ?

How many more come?

How many in all?

Count the ⬭'s in each box. Find the stickers that show how many ⬭'s in each box. Put each sticker next to the right box.

Skill: counting the members of two sets and finding the sticker with the correct total

Count the 's in each box. Find the stickers that show how many 's in each box. Put each sticker next to the right box.

How many in all?

sticker

sticker

sticker

sticker

Skill: counting the members of two sets and finding the sticker with the correct total

5

Count the animals in each row. How many in all?
Write the number in the box.

How many in all?

3

How many in all?

How many in all?

How many in all?

Skill: counting the members of two sets and writing the sum

Count the animals in each row. How many in all?
Write the number in the box.

How many in all? Write the number in the box.

8

How many in all? Write the number in the box.

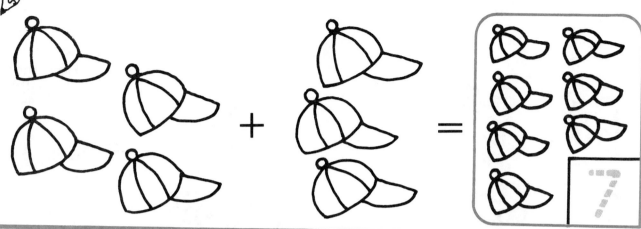

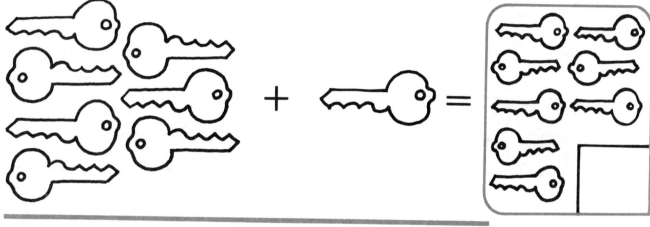

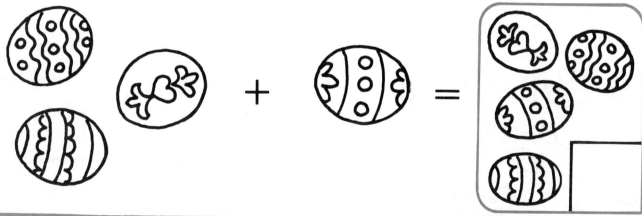

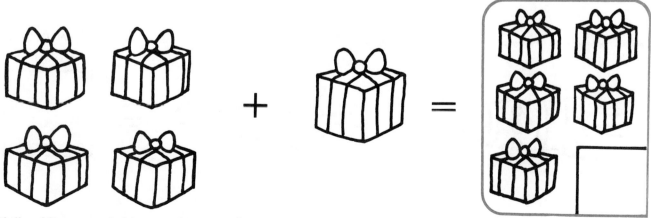

Count the objects in each row. How many in all? Write the number in the box.

 +  = **How many in all?**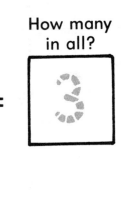

 +  = **How many in all?**

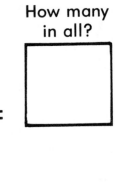 **How many in all?**

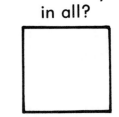 **How many in all?**

Skill: adding sets of objects and writing the sum

Count the objects in each row. How many in all? Write the number in the box.

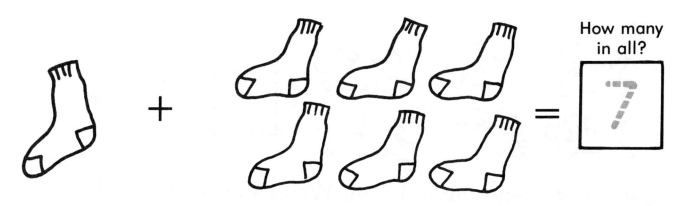

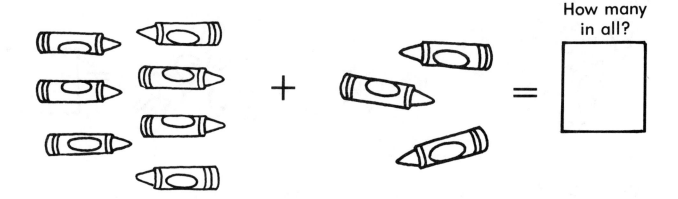

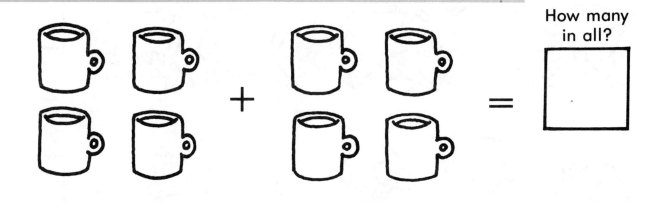

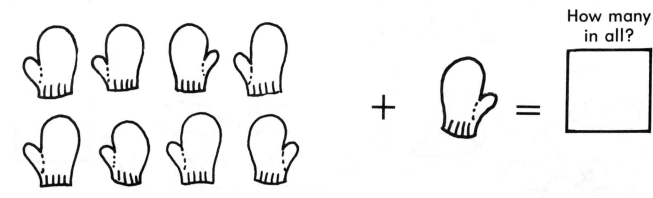

Count the 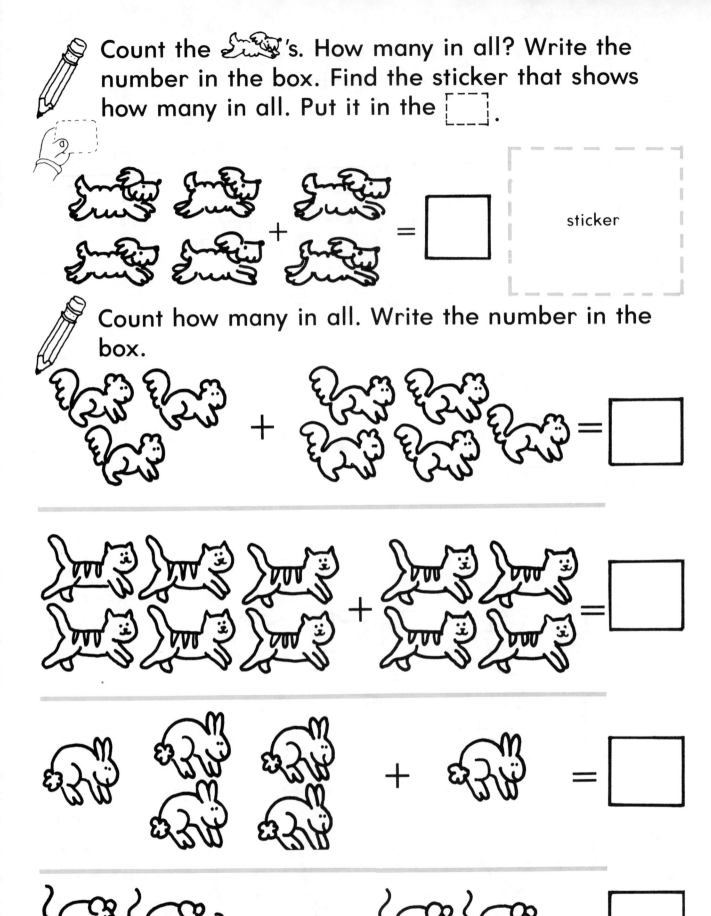's. How many in all? Write the number in the box. Find the sticker that shows how many in all. Put it in the ⬚.

Count how many in all. Write the number in the box.

Count how many in all. Write the number in the box.

 + = 8

 + = ☐

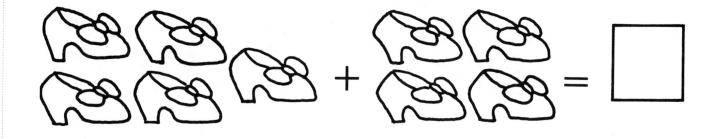 = ☐

 = ☐

Skill: adding sets of objects and writing the sum

13

Count the 🐦's in each group. Write the numbers. Add to find out how many in all.

How many in all?

$2 + 2 = 4$

How many in all?

☐ + ☐ = ☐

How many in all?

☐ + ☐ = ☐

Skill: adding sets of objects and writing the equation

Count the 's in each group. Write the numbers. Add to find out how many in all.

How many in all?

$$2 + 3 = 5$$

How many in all?

$$\square + \square = \square$$

How many in all?

$$\square + \square = \square$$

Count the 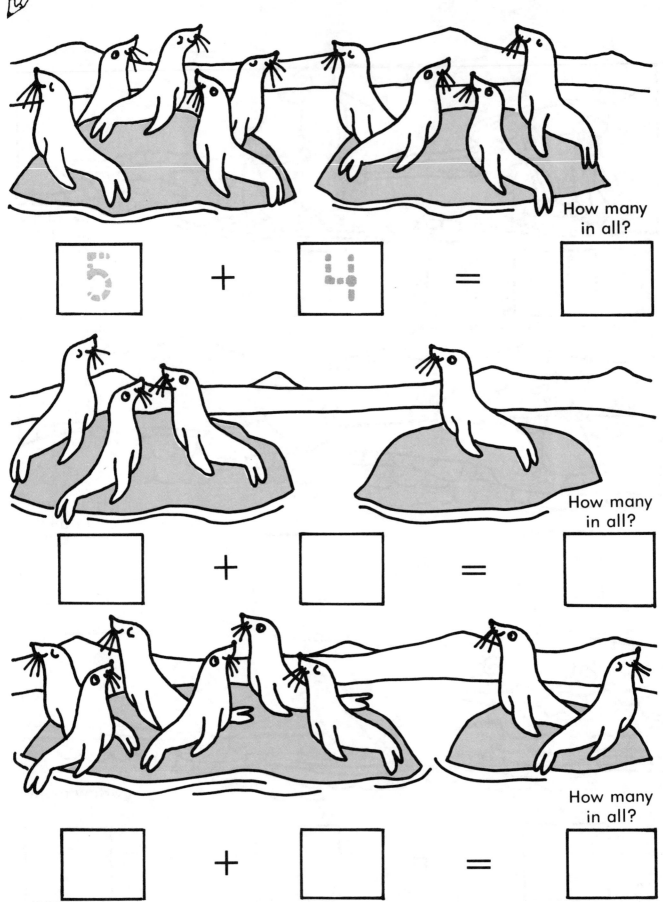's in each group. Write the numbers. Add to find out how many in all.

5 + 4 =   How many in all? ☐

☐ + ☐ = ☐   How many in all?

☐ + ☐ = ☐   How many in all?

16

Count the animals in each . Write the numbers. Find the sticker that shows how many in all. Put each sticker where it belongs.

4 + 4 = sticker

+ = sticker

+ = sticker

Skill: adding sets of objects and completing the equation

Count the objects in each group. Write the numbers. Add to find out how many in all.

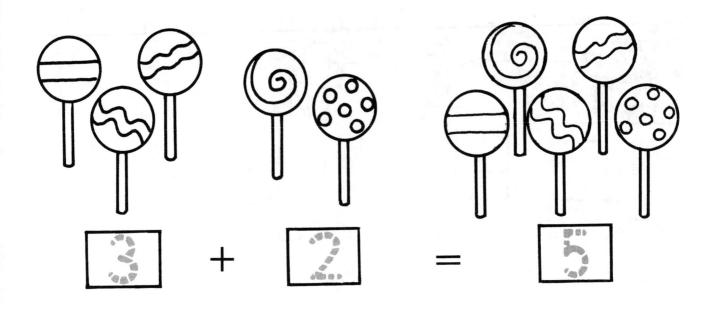

$$3 + 2 = 5$$

Find the sticker that shows the numbers. Put it in the ☐.

sticker

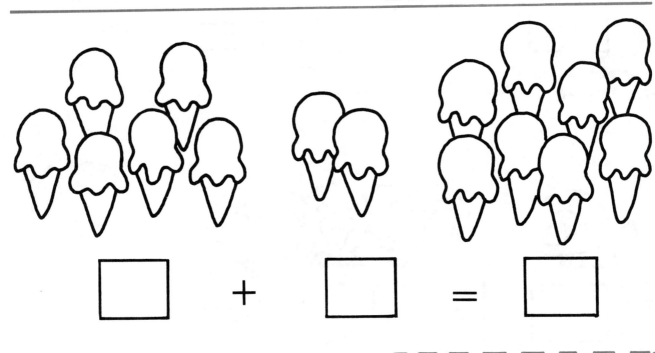

☐ + ☐ = ☐

sticker

Skill: adding sets of objects and writing the equation; finding the sticker with the matching equation

Count the objects in each group. Write the numbers. Add to find out how many in all.

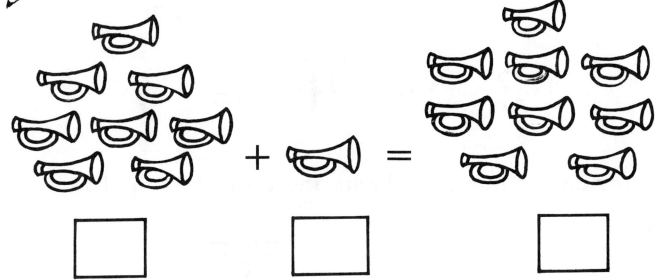

Find the sticker that shows
the numbers. Put it in the ☐.

sticker

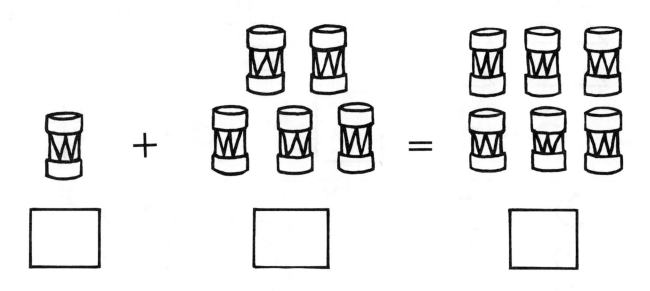

sticker

Find the stickers.

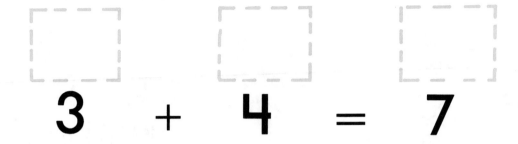

$$3 \quad + \quad 4 \quad = \quad 7$$

Add the numbers. Write the answer in the box.

○○ ○○

$2 + 2 = \boxed{4}$

$7 + 1 = \square$

$5 + 4 = \square$

$6 + 3 = \square$

$3 + 3 = \square$

$4 + 6 = \square$

<u>Skill</u>: adding sets of objects and completing the equation

Count the objects. Write the numbers. Add to find out how many in all.

2 + 4 = 6

☐ + ☐ = ☐

☐ + ☐ = ☐

☐ + ☐ = ☐

Count the objects. Write the numbers. Add to find out how many in all.

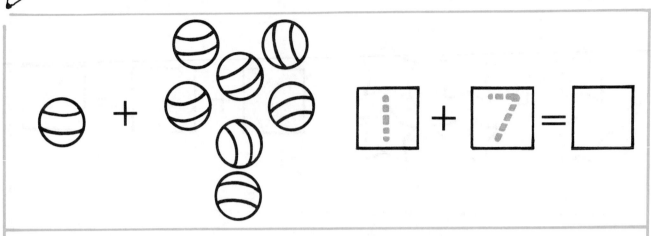

$$\boxed{1} + \boxed{7} = \boxed{}$$

$$\boxed{} + \boxed{} = \boxed{}$$

$$\boxed{} + \boxed{} = \boxed{}$$

$$\boxed{} + \boxed{} = \boxed{}$$

Skill: adding sets of objects and writing the equation

Add. Use your answers to find the hidden message below.

$5 + 1 =$ **B** 6	$2 + 3 =$ **R**
$7 + 2 =$ **E**	$5 + 3 =$ **T**
$1 + 1 =$ **G**	$3 + 1 =$ **O**
$5 + 2 =$ **J**	$9 + 1 =$ **A**

 Match each number in the hidden message to one of your answers. Write the letter on the line.

___ ___ ___ ___ ___
2   5   9   10   8

___ ___ B !
7   4   6

sticker

Skill: adding numbers to find the sum; solving a hidden message   23

Add the numbers. Write the answer in the box.
Find the 🐟 sticker with the same answer.
Put it on the 🐠.

4 + 3 = ☐   8 + 2 = ☐

sticker

sticker

6 + 2 = ☐   3 + 3 = ☐

sticker

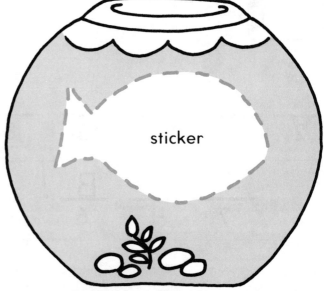

sticker

24   <u>Skill</u>: adding numbers to find the sum; finding the sticker with the matching sum

Add.

$$2 + 6 = 8$$

$$3 + 5 = 8 \qquad 1 + 9 = \square$$

$$2 + 7 = \square \qquad 4 + 5 = \square$$

$$6 + 1 = \square \qquad 8 + 2 = \square$$

$$7 + 3 = \square \qquad 3 + 3 = \square$$

Count the objects. Write the numbers. Add to find out how many in all.

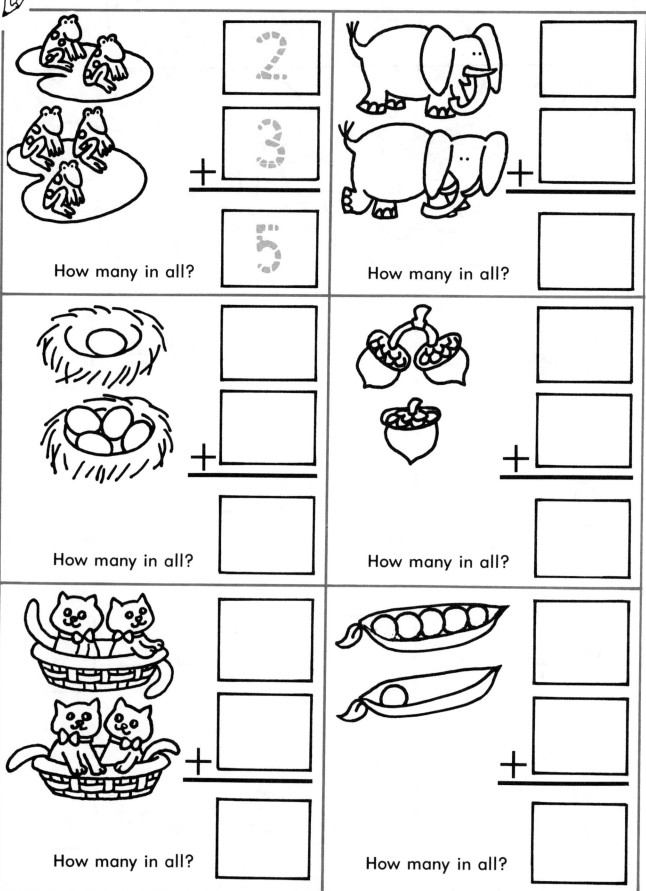

How many in all?

How many in all?

How many in all?

How many in all?

How many in all?

How many in all?

Skill: adding sets of objects and writing the equation in vertical form

Count the objects. Write the numbers. Add to find out how many in all.

2
4
+

6

How many in all?

How many in all?

+

How many in all?

+

How many in all?

+

How many in all?

+

How many in all?

+

How many in all?

Add.

7
+3
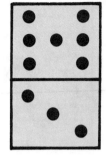

4
+5
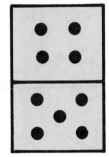

□

1
+8
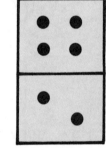

6
+1
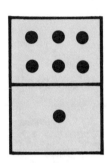

□

□

4
+2
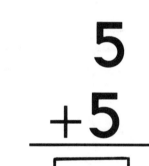

5
+5
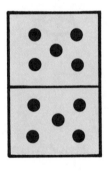

□

□

3
+5
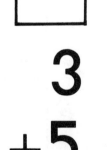

8
+2
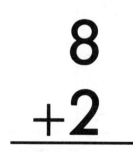

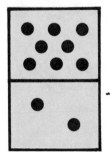

□

□

28

Skill: adding numbers to find the sum

Add.

$$\begin{array}{r} 2 \\ +5 \\ \hline 7 \end{array}$$

$$\begin{array}{r} 4 \\ +1 \\ \hline \boxed{5} \end{array}$$

$$\begin{array}{r} 6 \\ +3 \\ \hline \boxed{} \end{array}$$

$$\begin{array}{r} 2 \\ +5 \\ \hline \boxed{} \end{array}$$

$$\begin{array}{r} 4 \\ +5 \\ \hline \boxed{} \end{array}$$

$$\begin{array}{r} 9 \\ +1 \\ \hline \boxed{} \end{array}$$

$$\begin{array}{r} 3 \\ +4 \\ \hline \boxed{} \end{array}$$

Skill: adding numbers to find the sum

29

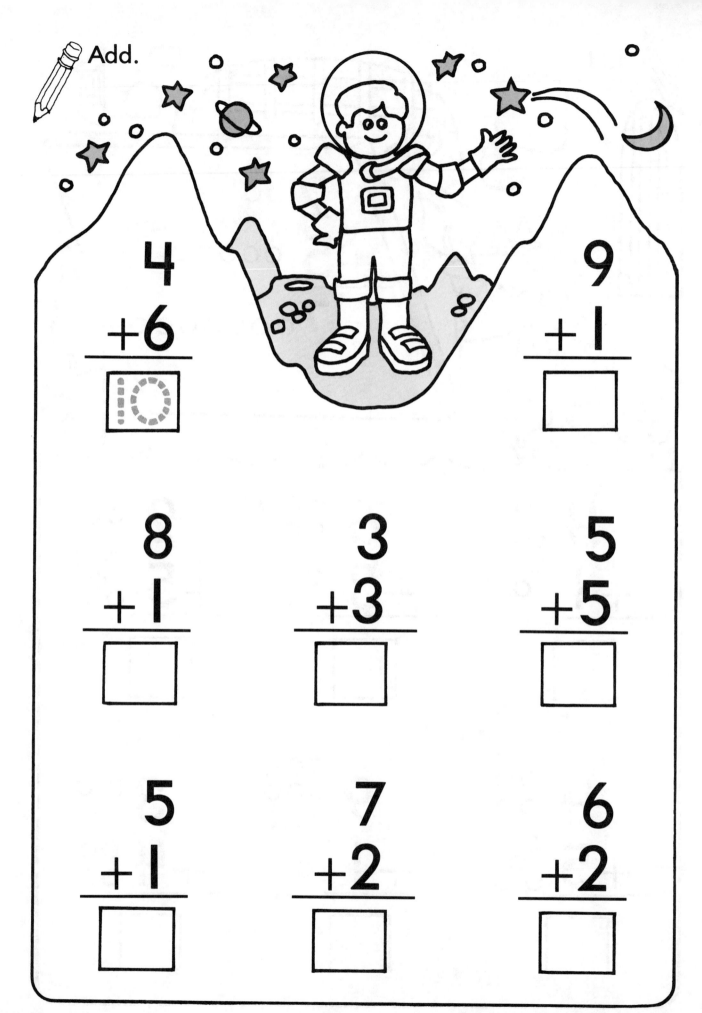

Add.

$$4$$
$$+6$$
$$\boxed{10}$$

$$9$$
$$+1$$
$$\boxed{}$$

$$8$$
$$+1$$
$$\boxed{}$$

$$3$$
$$+3$$
$$\boxed{}$$

$$5$$
$$+5$$
$$\boxed{}$$

$$5$$
$$+1$$
$$\boxed{}$$

$$7$$
$$+2$$
$$\boxed{}$$

$$6$$
$$+2$$
$$\boxed{}$$

30

Skill: adding numbers to find the sum

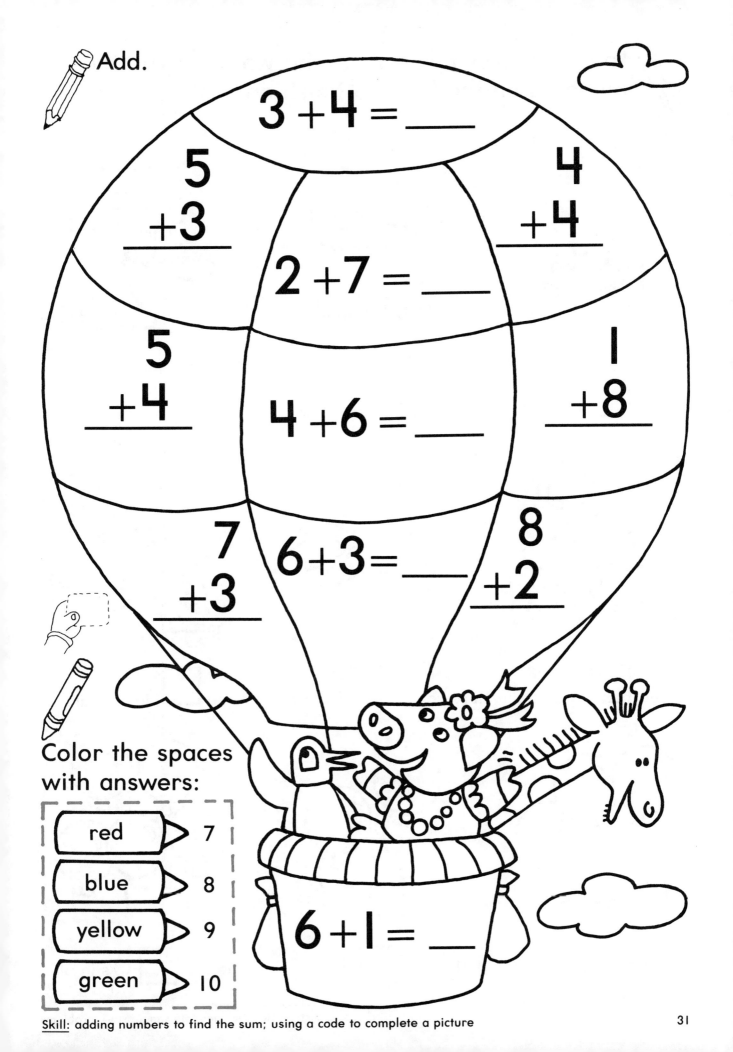

Add.

$3 + 4 =$ ___

5
$+3$
___

4
$+4$
___

$2 + 7 =$ ___

5
$+4$
___

$4 + 6 =$ ___

1
$+8$
___

7
$+3$
___

$6 + 3 =$ ___

8
$+2$
___

Color the spaces
with answers:

red ▷ 7

blue ▷ 8

yellow ▷ 9

green ▷ 10

$6 + 1 =$ ___

Skill: adding numbers to find the sum; using a code to complete a picture

31

Look at the pictures. Read the words. Write the numbers on the lines to finish each story.

☐ bug.

☐ more bugs.

☐ bugs in all.

I see ☐ dogs.

Here comes ☐ more.

I see ☐ dogs in all.

He has ☐ 🎈's.

He gets ☐ more.

He has ☐ 🎈's in all.

Skill: using picture clues to complete simple story problems

pages 18-19

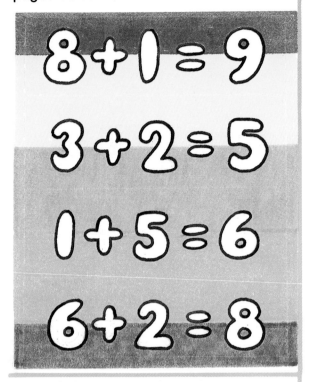

$$8 + 1 = 9$$
$$3 + 2 = 5$$
$$1 + 5 = 6$$
$$6 + 2 = 8$$

page 24

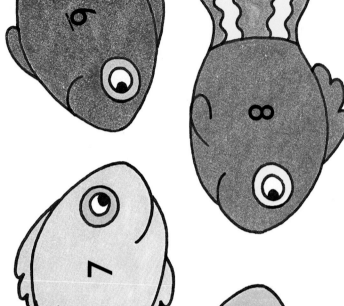

page 20

page 23

Rewards!

Use these stickers as rewards on any page.

page 31

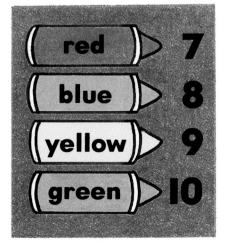

red	7
blue	8
yellow	9
green	10